the 4th Garfield
TREASURY

the 4th Garfield TREASURY

BY: JIM DAVIS

BALLANTINE BOOKS • NEW YORK

Copyright © 1987 United Feature Syndicate, Inc. All rights reserved.

All rights reserved under International and Pan-American Copyright Conventions. Published in the United States by Ballantine Books, a division of Random House, Inc., New York, and simultaneously in Canada by Random House of Canada Limited, Toronto.

The Sunday strips appearing here in color were previously included in black and white in GARFIELD Rolls On, GARFIELD Out to Lunch, GARFIELD Food for Thought, and GARFIELD Swallows His Pride.

Library of Congress Catalog Card Number: 86-92102

ISBN: 0-345-34726-9

Manufactured in the United States of America

First Edition: November 1987

10 9 8 7

PUCUCK!

ONE MORE STUNT LIKE THAT AND I'M GOING TO WRING YOUR RUBBER CHICKEN'S NECK!

I'M SORRY I SNAPPED AT YOU, GARFIELD. WILL YOU FORGIVE ME?

I FORGIVE YOU

SMACK!

WHAP!

BUT STRETCH DOESN'T!

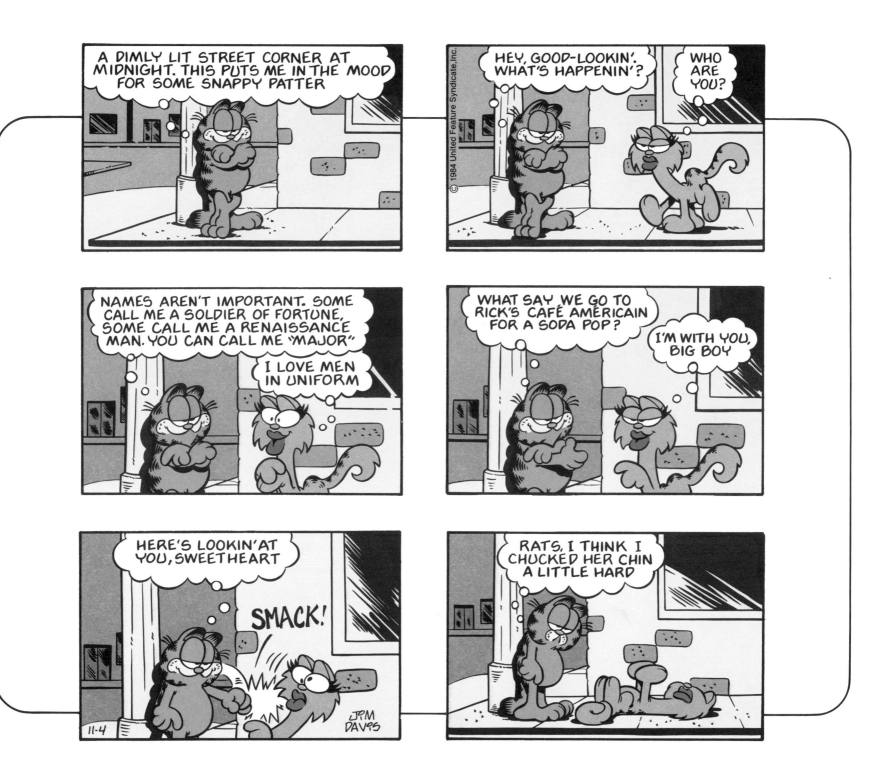

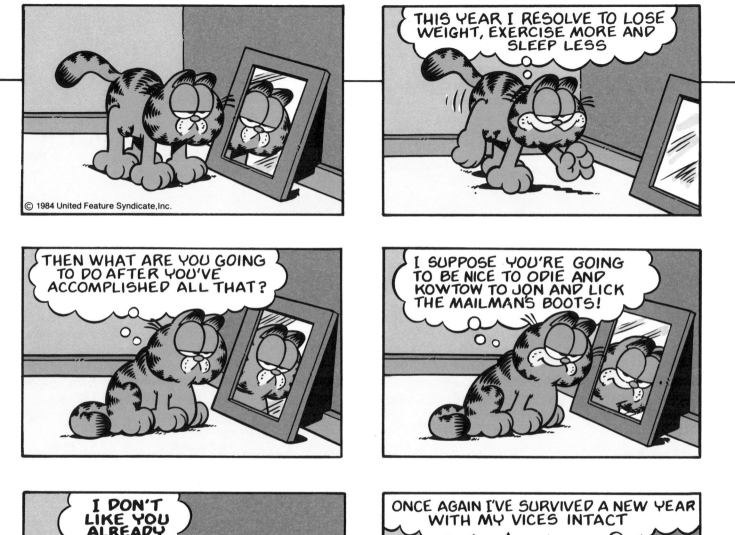

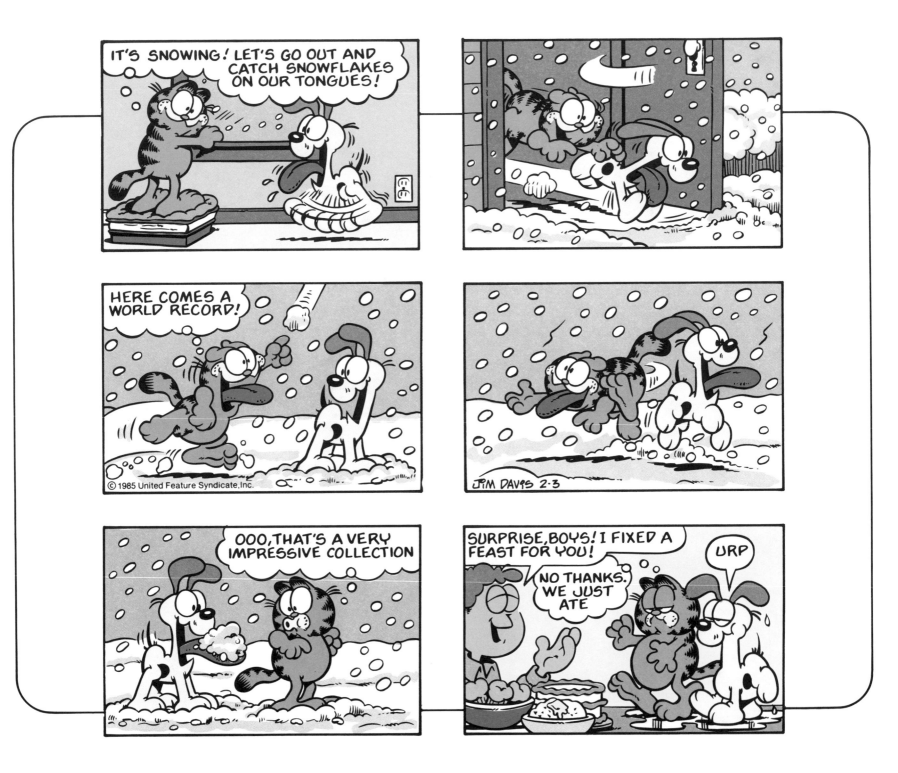

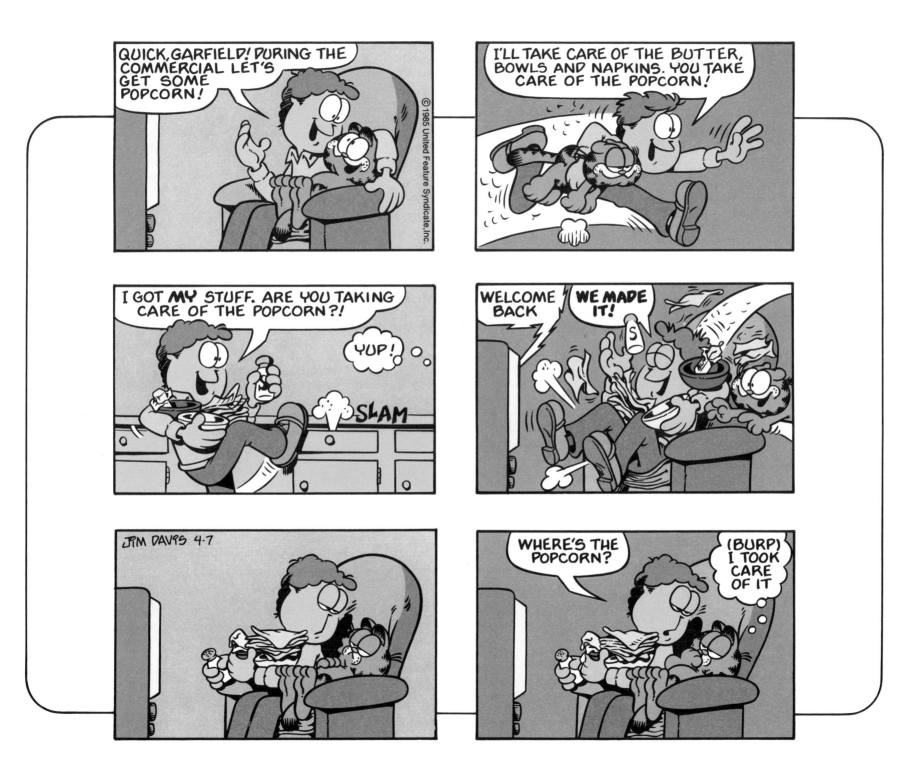

© 1985 United Feature Syndicate, Inc.

JRM DAVIS 4-21

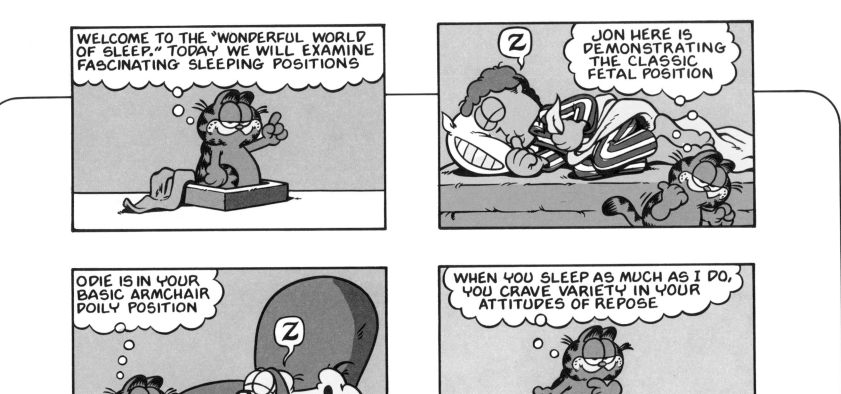

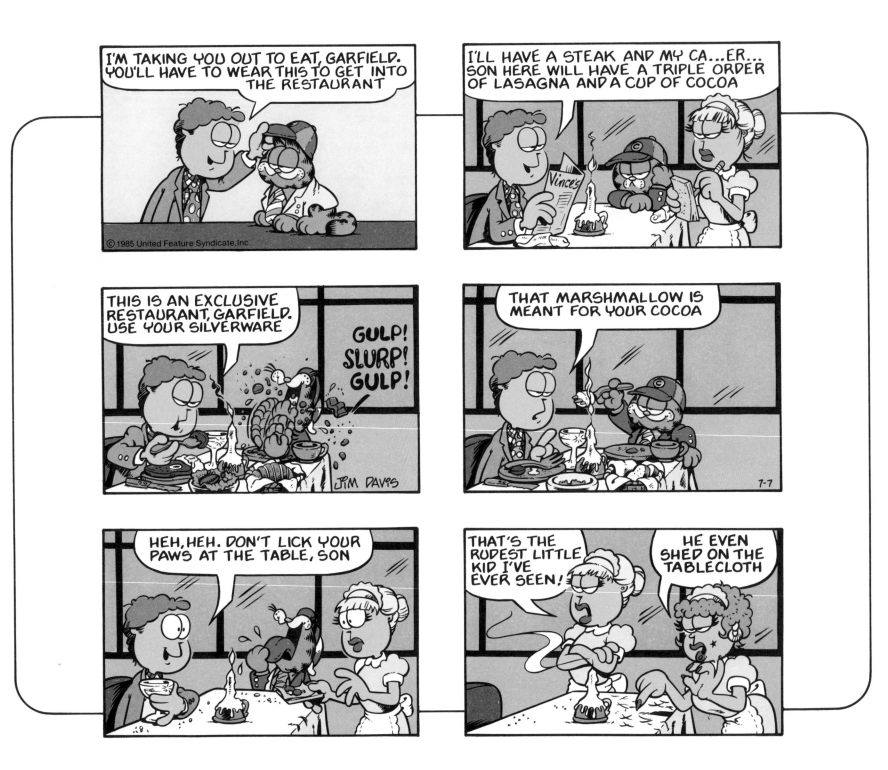

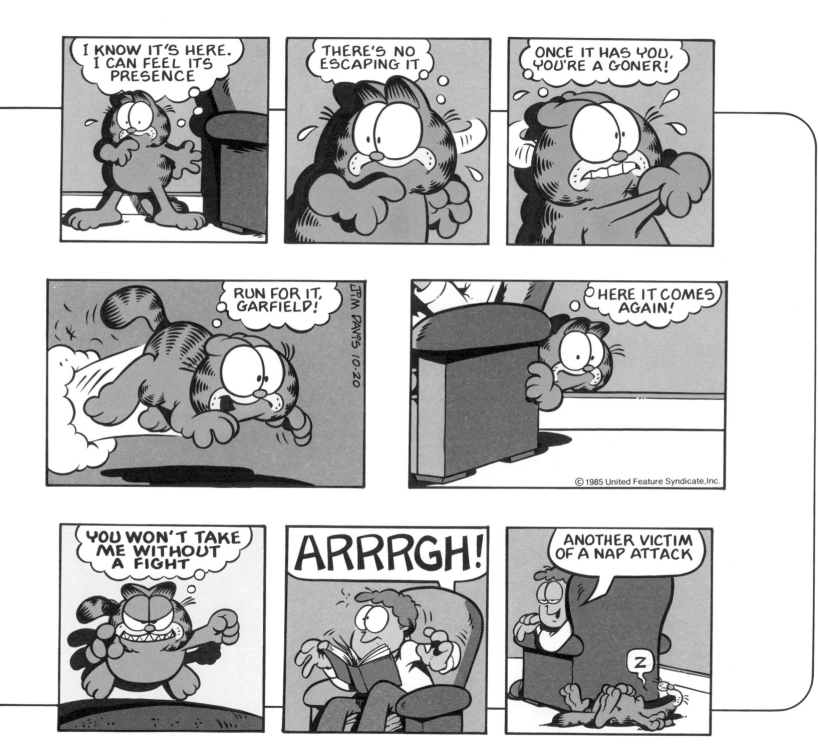

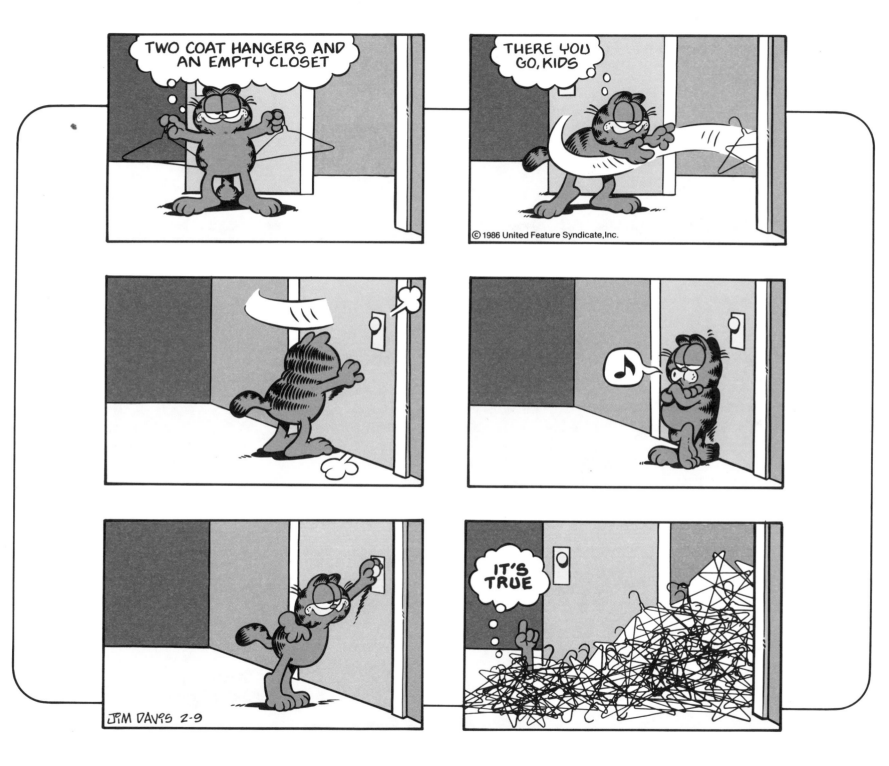

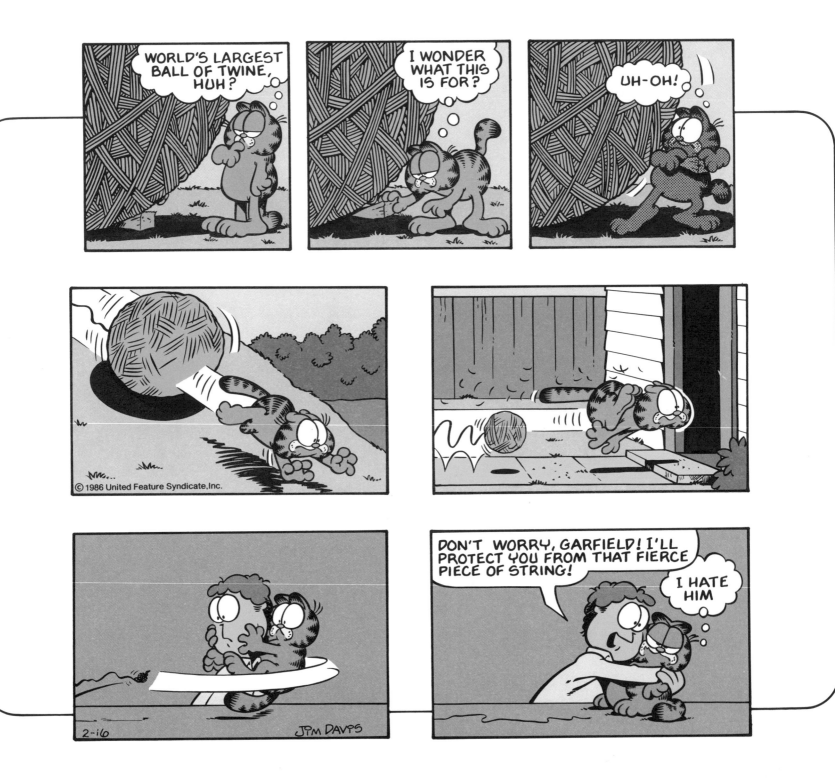

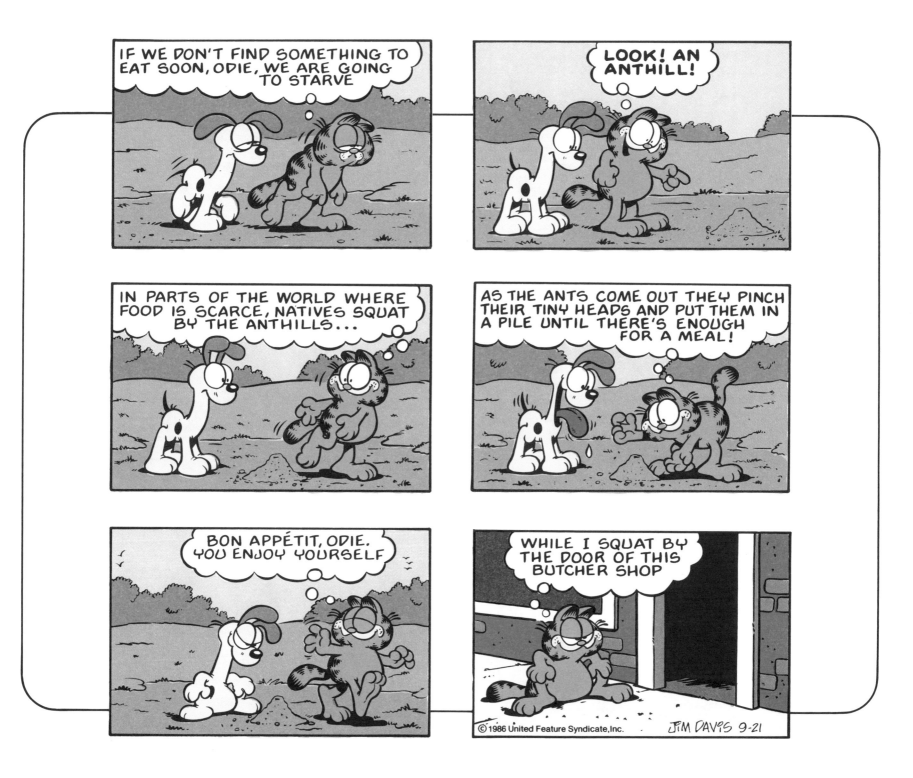

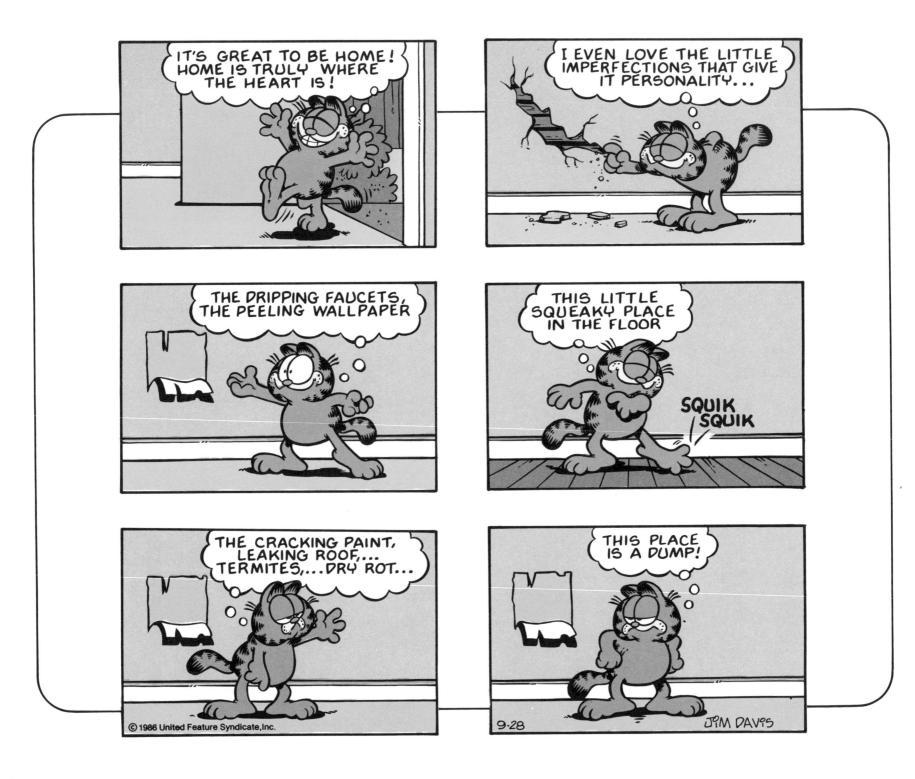

JIM DAVIS 11-9

How the Garfield Sunday Strip is Produced

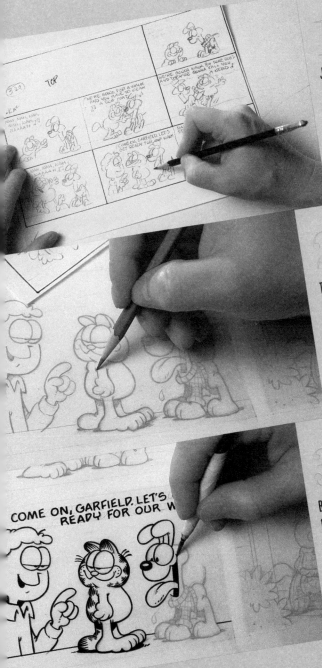

1 Jim writes the comic strip and draws a rough or "thumb-nail" version of it.

2 The thumbnail is used as a guide to draw the actual comic strip with a blue pencil. This drawing is called the "blueline."

3 Black ink and a brush are then used to draw over the blueline, and a pen is used to do the lettering.

4 A copy of the black and white comic strip is colored so the printer will know how it should look in your newspaper.

5 Jim approves, signs and dates the finished strip, and it's shipped to United Feature Syndicate for printing and distribution.

6 Twelve weeks later, you get to read GARFIELD in your Sunday paper.

HEY THIS CAT IS FUNNY!

BIRTHDAYS, HOLIDAYS, OR ANY DAY . . .

Keep GARFIELD on your calendar all year 'round!

GARFIELD TV SPECIALS
__BABES & BULLETS   36339/$6.95
__A GARFIELD CHRISTMAS   34368/$6.95
__GARFIELD GOES HOLLYWOOD   34580/$6.95
__GARFIELD'S HALLOWEEN ADVENTURE   33045/$6.95
  (formerly GARFIELD In Disguise)
__GARFIELD'S FELINE FANTASIES   36903/$6.95
__GARFIELD IN PARADISE   33796/$6.95
__GARFIELD IN THE ROUGH   32242/$6.95
__GARFIELD ON THE TOWN   31542/$6.95
__A GARFIELD THANKSGIVING   35650/$6.95
__HERE COMES GARFIELD   32012/$6.95

BALLANTINE SALES
Dept. TA, 201 E. 50th St., New York, N.Y. 10022

Please send me the BALLANTINE BOOKS I have checked above. I am enclosing $ .... (add $2.00 for the first book and 50¢ for each additional book to cover postage and handling). Send check or money order—no cash or C.O.D.'s please. Prices are subject to change without notice.

GREETINGS FROM GARFIELD!
GARFIELD POSTCARD BOOKS FOR ALL OCCASIONS.
__#1 THINKING OF YOU   36516/$6.95
__#2 WORDS TO LIVE BY   36679/$6.95
__#3 GARFIELD BIRTHDAY GREETINGS   36770/$7.95
__#4 BE MY VALENTINE   37121/$7.95

Also from GARFIELD:
__GARFIELD: HIS NINE LIVES   32061/$9.95
__THE GARFIELD BOOK OF CAT NAMES   35082/$5.95
__THE GARFIELD TRIVIA BOOK   33771/$5.95
__THE UNABRIDGED UNCENSORED
  UNBELIEVABLE GARFIELD   33772/$5.95
__GARFIELD: THE ME BOOK   36545/$7.95
__GARFIELD'S JUDGMENT DAY   36755/$6.95

Name _____

Address _____

City_____ State_____ Zip Code_____
30   Allow at least 4 weeks for delivery   3/90 TA-267